HUMAN BODY

D1285023

KINGFISHER

KINGFISHER

First published 2011 by Kingfisher
an imprint of Macmillan Children's Books
a division of Macmillan Publishers Limited
20 New Wharf Road, London N1 9RR
Basingstoke and Oxford
Associated companies throughout the world
www.panmacmillan.com

ISBN 978-0-7534-3082-8

Consultant: Dougal Hargreaves

Designed and created by Basher www.basherbooks.com
Text written by Dan Green

Dedicated to Jean and Colette Rollet

Text and design copyright © Toucan Books Ltd. 2011
Based on an original concept by Toucan Books Ltd.
Illustrations copyright © Simon Basher 2011

9 8 7 6 5 4 3 2 1
1TR/1010/WKT/UNTD/140MA

A CIP catalogue record for this book
is available from the British Library.

Printed in China

Note to readers: the website addresses listed above are correct at
the time of going to print. However, due to the ever-changing nature
of the internet, website addresses and content can change. Websites
can contain links that are unsuitable for children. The publisher cannot
be held responsible for changes in website addresses or content, or for
information obtained through a third party. We strongly advise that
internet searches should be supervised by an adult.

CONTENTS

Introduction

Human Body

Your body is a most amazing machine. It is armed with multi-tool-kit hands, propelled by two legs and governed by a brain capable of independent thought (well, sometimes), speech and problem-solving. Supertough on the outside – think skin, hair, nails – your insides house all the delicate organs and impressively sophisticated body systems that keep you in perfect shape.

Though you are undoubtedly gorgeous to look at, most of your best bits are hidden from view. Anatomy bod Andreas Vesalius (1514–64) decided to take a look for himself. It was a grisly job that involved dissecting the odd cadaver (dead body to you) and rummaging around inside. He stuck it out, though, making detailed drawings, and discovered that all sorts of accepted "facts" about the human body were actually wrong. For example, he dispelled the myth that women have one rib more than men. He also found that the liver had just two lobes and not five, as suspected. Thanks to him, we know so much more about our bodies now and the mind-blowing life beneath our skin. Well, come on, let's get in there...

Andreas Vesalius

Man and Woman

* Adult members of the species *Homo sapiens sapiens*
* The same kind of living thing, but each with subtle differences
* Like other mammal females, Woman gives birth to live young

Make way, the humans are coming! We are a daring duo, powerful beasts, striding out on two legs. We are the same animal, but exist as either Man or Woman. And when we get together sparks really fly, for together we make Baby.

Man is the taller, more muscle-y variety. He wears his sex organs on the outside, and his teenage body changes are fuelled by the hormone testosterone. Woman's sex organs are tucked away inside her body so that she can nurture Baby for nine months. The female hormone, oestrogen, triggers a different set of body changes that allow her to do this. Our gender is determined by two chromosomes called "X" and "Y" – two Xs for a female, and an X and a Y for a male. Only Man carries a Y, so it's down to him as to which mini-version of us you get to be!

● Tallest human: Robert Wadlow (2.72 m)
● Oldest human: Jeanne Calment (122 years and 164 days; 1875–1997)
● Average weight: 76–83 kg (Man); 54–64 kg (Woman)

Man and Woman

Baby

* This young imp is the offspring of Man and Woman
* Born after around 40 weeks' gestation in Woman's body
* Infant babies drink milk produced by their mothers

I am the pinnacle of creation. Life's greatest little trick. I start out as one unimaginably small cell, when Man's sperm combines with Woman's egg: the moment of fertilization. Nine months later, I pop out – that big-headed, chubby, wailing, feeding and pooing machine you just can't help loving! Ahh. Coochy-coo!

I'm pretty helpless in the beginning. My skull still has soft spots, called fontanelles. They don't harden to bone for months. I can only focus on things about 30 cm away, but that's fine 'cos, mostly, I'm breastfeeding. I smile from about six weeks, but it takes me nine months to crawl and a year to master the coordination and balance for walking. Speaking is really hard and it might be twelve months before I utter my first word. But once I start…

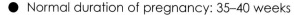

● Normal duration of pregnancy: 35–40 weeks
● Average weight at birth: 3.2 kg
● Average length at birth: 35.6–50.8 cm

Baby

Chapter 1
Body Building Blocks

It all starts with these tiny tots. Before you became a running, jumping, eating, breathing, speaking, bad-smell-making all-round hero, you were an insignificant microdot of cells. Here then, for your delight and entertainment, are the bunch of microscopic marvels that make up wonderful you! It all starts with Cell, whose eight guises make up Tissue. Then you've got your bone-builders, your muscle-makers, your fetch-and-carry men, your defence team and your sense centres. Don't miss this once-in-a-lifetime chance to lift the lid on your body and see what goes on inside. Go on, take a peek if you dare!

Cell

DNA

Gene

Mitochondrion

Protein

Stem Cell

Sperm

Egg

Nerve Cell

Red Blood Cell

White Blood Cells

Osteoblast

Body Tissue

Cell
Body Building Blocks

- A tiny unit of living matter inside a membrane
- It's all go in this chemical factory that runs your body
- Eight basic types of specialist cell make up the human body

All great things come in small packages and I'm no exception. I am *the* definitive building block. Everything that happens in your body happens because of me. I might be small, but I'm no lightweight, I can assure you!

Put me under the microscope and you'll see what I mean. Inside my cool plasma membrane, I'm busy working with all sorts of chemicals to make everything you need to keep your body functioning. Dig a little deeper and you'll find my nucleus. This limited-access area is my control centre and home to your genius gene-giving DNA.

I don't like to work alone, though. It takes millions of me to make up your whole body. I divide to make copies of myself so there are always enough of me to go round.

- Average size: 0.01–0.03 mm
- No. of cells in a fertilized egg: 1
- No. of cells in a human body: 50,000 billion to 100 trillion

Cell

DNA
Body Building Blocks

* Found in almost every cell in your body
* Can be used to identify an individual, just like a fingerprint
* Only identical twins have *exactly* the same DNA

It's hard not to feel important when your name is Deoxyribonucleic Acid and, dare I say it, I am a rather special chemical compound. You see, I hold the key to the very secret of life!

I am a learned fellow known as a double helix. My two sleek strands are chemically linked together like a ladder and spiralled like a corkscrew. My bases (the ladder rungs) are made from just four substances, but in long sequences they make a complex code that tells your body how to work. My home is Cell's nucleus, where 46 strips of me are arranged in 23 pairs called chromosomes. I'm like a blueprint for who you are. And whenever Cell divides, I make an exact copy of myself so that all your cells carry the same code. Face it, without me, you wouldn't be you.

● No. of different chromosomes in the body: 46 (in 23 pairs)
● No. of bases in a chromosome: 50 million to 280 million
● DNA discoverer: Friedrich Miescher (1869)

DNA

Gene
Body Building Blocks

* A small portion of DNA on a chromosome
* Genes tell the body how to build or operate its bits
* Your genes are passed on to you from both parents

Are you clumsy, like your Dad? Tone deaf, like your Mum? Blame little old me. I'm a how-to guide for the human body – the instructions for making, running and maintaining body parts. I'm crucial to your appearance and natural abilities, because your body's cells use me to build bits such as your brain, skin, hair, eyes and nose. I come in pairs – one set from Mum and one from Dad.

I'm unbelievably tiny: inside Cell's nucleus are 46 strands of DNA, tightly curled up. These are called chromosomes. Straighten them all out and they'd stretch almost 3 metres and contain about 50,000 of me! Small sequences of DNA signal the end of one gene and the start of another so that a chromosome can be understood – just as a capital letter and a full stop give sense to sentences. Gene-ius!

● Genetic similarity between humans: 99.998 %
● Genetic similarity between a human and a mouse: 92 %
● No. of genes on a chromosome: up to 3000

Gene

Mitochondrion
Body Building Blocks

* The pocket rocket – the power supply inside your cells
* A torpedo-shaped hot rod that dismantles cells when they die
* DNA in mitochondria is passed on through your mother

Fast and furious, I'm the little guy who generates Cell's power. And it's no mean feat! I whizz about (there are millions of us) making a fuel called ATP. It's full of life-giving energy and ready whenever Cell needs some juice. The more she wants, the more we make. And when demand threatens to outstrip supply, we simply divide and multiply to increase our output.

Mitochondrion

● Size: 0.0005–0.01 mm
● No. of genes: 37
● ATP production: 5 million per second

Protein

Body Building Blocks

- ✷ Long chains of amino acids arranged in fixed sequences
- ✷ Groups of chemicals that include enzymes and blood cells
- ✷ Protein chains have shapes that relate to their function

Protein

I'm a busy-body, a doer, a jack-of-all trades. My funky, chain-like form gets made inside your cells. It's built from amino acids that are absorbed from food and arranged in different sequences. You'll find me knocking about in every corner of your body. And, boy, am I keen, just waiting for an opportunity to help digest your food, carry oxygen to your cells and keep your health tiptop.

- ● No. of amino acids in the body: 20
- ● Keratin: a protein found in skin, hair and nails
- ● Elastin: a protein found in skin and arteries

Stem Cell

Body Building Blocks

- A cell with fantastic morphing potential
- Found in embryos, bone marrow, the liver and the brain
- Could be used for growing replacement body bits

I am the cell with infinite potential, the Special One, have no doubt! There's no other cell quite like me, because I can become any type of cell that takes my fancy. My cellular cousins start and end life as specialists – in the brain or skin, for example – but me, I'm a mighty morpher.

I'm not just boasting! My unique shape-shifting talents make me incredibly valuable. Just think about it: because I can divide to become anything from kidney cells to muscle or heart cells, I could one day be used to create custom-built organs for transplants. So how do I do it? Well, I multiply, just like Cell does. But when *I* split, each new cell gets to choose whether to stay the same or become something different. Mmm, let's see... Nerve Cell? Nah... Muscle Cell...? Maybe...

- No. of different types of cell a stem cell can become: 220
- Most common stem cells: located in 3- to 5-day-old embryo
- Adult stem cells: found mostly in bone marrow and skin

Stem Cell

Sperm
Body Building Blocks

* One of millions that race to fertilize an egg
* This swimming champ carries only a half-set of DNA
* Carries an X or a Y chromosome to decide the sex of a baby

On your marks. Get set. Go! I'm called a spermatozoon, but I prefer spermatozoom, 'cos I'm one speedy kinda guy. Lovely Egg and I make new life.

I'm a little guy with a big job and my life is brief but glorious. Starting from the testes, a man's sperm factory, I travel upstream towards the penis. I pick up fluids as I pass the prostate gland, and these give me fuel for my journey. If everything goes "swimmingly", I enter the female body and whip my long tail for the hour's swim to my eggy destination. Sounds easy? Are you kidding? It's a real challenge. First, I have to reach Egg before she gets too old (believe me, it's a small window). Second, I have to race against several million of my own kind. There's no denying it, you've gotta have bottle!

● Swimming speed: 1–3 mm per minute
● No. of sperm produced per day: 50 million to 500 million
● Length of sperm head: 0.05 mm

Sperm

Egg
Body Building Blocks

- The largest cell made by the human body
- A woman releases just 400 of these cells in a lifetime
- The female sex cell – its proper name is ovum

Graceful and gorgeous, I ripen in a woman's ovary just once a month. Like a tiny bubble, I float dreamily down the Fallopian tube, hoping that speedy Sperm is on his way to see me.

I'm an easy target – 85,000 times larger than Sperm in terms of volume – so his chances of finding me should be pretty high. Each of us has a half-set of DNA, and if Sperm makes it, these fuse to create a brand-new being. Then, deep within the protection of the uterus, I start to grow into Baby. It's awesome, but there is a catch; we simply don't have much time. Within just 24 hours of starting my journey, I will have grown too old for that all-important date. And if Sperm doesn't show up? I exit, during a period, so that another Egg can try in four weeks' time.

- Diameter of fertilized egg: 0.15 mm
- Lifespan after release: 24 hours
- Time a fertilized egg takes to grow into a baby: 35–40 weeks

Egg

Nerve Cell
Body Building Blocks

* Your central nervous system acts on messages from your brain
* There are approximately 100 billion nerve cells in the brain
* Controls automatic functions, such as breathing and sweating

I am a real live wire, a special type of cell that passes messages from all parts of your body to your brain. I help you to sense the world around you, move about and feel pain. That's me – highly charged and ready for action.

You are, quite literally, one big bag of nerves. I'm joined together in long chains that connect you up from head to toe. Each one of me has tiny thread-like extensions, called fibres, that make me extra-specially touchy-feely. I'm like a super-efficient network of shiny wires with electrical signals speeding along me like greased lightning!

Brain likes to order me about, but there are some things I control automatically – like regulating your body temperature – so you never have to think about them.

* Width of nerve fibre: 0.01 mm
* Strength of nerve signal: more than 30 millivolts (mV)
* Average nerve signal length: 0.001 seconds

Nerve Cell

Red Blood Cell
Body Building Blocks

- A cell made in your bone marrow
- This ruddy roustabout carries oxygen around your body
- One drop of blood contains 250 million of these blusterers

Forever young, I'm a specialist trained to bring life-giving oxygen to Cell. Duty calls me whenever and wherever I'm needed. Call me a doughnut if you like – I'm shaped like one and, with no genes of my own, I'm a simple kind of guy – but I perform a vital task.

Just one of me can carry a billion oxygen molecules! I use an iron-rich chemical called haemoglobin to pick up oxygen as I travel through the lungs with Blood. It's an exhausting task, and in about 120 days (and nearly 1000 blood-soaked kilometres), I've just about had it.

No easy retirement for me, though. Liver breaks me down and I get flushed out of the body in urine. My lovely red colour becomes the yellow in your wee. What a wash-out!

- Average size: 0.007 mm
- No. of red blood cells in the body: 25 trillion
- Red blood cell discoverer: Jan Swammerdam, 1658

Red Blood Cell

White Blood Cells
Body Building Blocks

- Blood cells that form part of your immune system
- These guys go by the proper name of leucocytes
- The little critters increase in number to fight off disease

Meet the White Blood Cell squad, an elite unit in your bloodstream. "To serve and protect" is our motto and we live and die by it. Our mission? To seek and destroy.

Five of us operate in this tight outfit, each with his own jurisdiction. We roam your body looking for creeps and lowlifes who barge in uninvited. Bacteria, viruses, cancer cells – you name them, we're onto them. Neutrophil targets infections that invade through broken skin. Basophil triggers allergic-response chemicals. Eosinophil stalks parasites and Monocyte mops up debris. Heading up the crew is Lymphocyte, aka Captain Immunity. He kills off body-cells-gone-bad and protects against future disease. Unlike most of the WBC squad, who last only hours or days, Lymphocyte can live for a few years.

- Proportion of WBCs in blood: 0.7 %
- No. of WBCs in body: 20–55 billion
- Breakdown: neutro. (62 %), lympho. (27 %), mono. (6 %), eosino. (4 %), baso. (1 %)

White Blood Cells

Osteoblast

Body Building Blocks

* Bone-making cell generated by stem cells in the bone marrow
* Your body uses this guy to fix broken bones
* This hard cell dies off in elderly people

A tough little hard hat, I am a foundation stone of the bone construction business. Without me and my pals, the whole industry would collapse (taking you with it)! So if you've never heard of me before, you'd better bone up!

I lay down calcium phosphate, the rock-hard stuff that makes your skeleton. Some collagen goes into the mix, too. This keeps your bones a little flexible and makes them less brittle. Highly specialized, I make two types of bone. The first is spongy and forms a honeycomb mesh down Bone's centre. It's rammed with wobbly-jelly bone marrow. The second is compact – literally thousands of us huddled tight together – and is used to make Bone's tough outer sheath. I'm always at it, constantly replacing the cells in your bones – never call me bone idle!

● Strongest bone in the body: thigh bone (femur)
● Bone is four times lighter than steel
● About one-seventh of total body weight is bone

Osteoblast

Body Tissue
Body Building Blocks

* Made from layers of similar cells working together
* All the functional parts of your body are made from tissue
* Important tissues are bone, fat, collagen, muscle and blood

I am the fabulously sloppy stuff that fills your holes and holds you together. When it comes to building your body, humdrum Cell may start the job, but it's definitely *me* who finishes it. Honestly, she'd be nothing on her own!

I am the innard wizard! Call me a smarm-ball, but I can't help it. I ooze class, as I arrange Cell into different groups and layers to make all your gorgeously gloopy insides. Gristle, sinew, marrow, your muscle, your fat and your slippery membranes – these are all down to me and my meticulous organization. Even those self-satisfied, puffed-up, complex organs like Heart, Kidney and Skin are made simply by combining layers of my various, wonderfully unctuous functional units. Now that's what I call "organ"-ized!

● Types of tissue: connective, muscle, nervous, epithelial
● Connective tissue: bone, blood and collagen
● Epithelial tissue: skin

Body Tissue

Chapter 2
Musculoskeletal Meatheads

Let's have some respect for this upstanding crew! Without these bods you'd be a jelly-like lump on the floor. They're the guys who give you shape, put steel into your body and get you moving about. First off there's Bone, who makes up your skeleton. Spine and thick Skull are part of his set-up, providing you with all that super-strength and protection. Then you've got Skeletal Muscle. Frankly, he's the one that sets it all in motion. He'd find it hard without Cartilage, though, who ties your bones together at their creaking joints. But, hey, come on and meet this upright crowd – it's a "moving" experience!

Bone

Skeletal Muscle

Cartilage

Skull

Spine

Bone

■ Musculoskeletal Meatheads

☀ This hard case forms your internal skeleton
☀ A living organ made up of different cells and supplied by blood
☀ Of the 206 bones in your body, 106 are in your hands and feet

Hard as they come, I'm your bodyguard, your knight in shining armour. As Skull, I protect your vulnerable brain, and, as ribs, I help shelter your heart and lungs.

I'm made of pretty stern stuff, me, from the longest bone in your thigh (femur) to the smallest bone in your ear (stirrup). I make up the complex framework on which you hang your organs. You use me like a set of levers to heave about your limbs. Make no bones about it, without me, you'd be nothing more than a crumpled heap of flesh. Ouch! You'd think I was dead but I am very much alive, I can assure you. Ask those Osteoblasts who do my maintenance. They're always making more of me to help you grow bigger, and they patch me up when I break. I can stick around for a thousand years without rotting.

● Weight of an adult skeleton: about 14 % of total body weight
● No. of ribs in a human body: 24 (in 12 pairs)
● One in 200 people have an extra rib or two

Bone

Skeletal Muscle

■ Musculoskeletal Meatheads

✳ A main body tissue, this meathead loves to move it
✳ Bundles of protein fibres, joined to the bones by tendons
✳ One of three muscle brothers (with cardiac and smooth)

Pay no attention to gloating Bone – it's me that keeps you up. I'm the muscle behind your every move, got it? The expressions "bone idle", "lazybones" and "bonehead" haven't come out of thin air – Bone is all talk and no action, and you heard it here first!

Just look at me. I'm a bulked-up, boisterous body-builder that makes up about 40 per cent of your body weight. I work hard, but my long ropey fibres can only pull in one direction, so I work in pairs. One bunch bends while the other bunch straightens. My length shortens as I pull, which is why I bulge when I tighten. I need to be big to support and move Bone about, but I can also make myself small for fine, controlled movements like writing or raising an eyebrow. Hey, I'm not a total meathead!

● No. of muscles in the human body: about 639
● Fastest muscle movements: those controlling the eye (200–400 milliseconds)
● No. of muscles used for walking: more than 200

Skeletal Muscle

Cartilage
■ Musculoskeletal Meatheads

✳ One of the body's main connective tissues
✳ Less flexible than muscle, but not as hard as bone
✳ Your nose and the outer parts of your ear are made of this

Hail the ultimate middle man, the mighty connector. Soft and pliable, I'm your flexible friend. I'll bend over backwards to help you walk, twist, jump, sit and dance.

Face it, you'd be as stiff as a board if you were made from hardman Bone alone. He's so tough, he doesn't *do* bending. Something's gotta give, and that's where I come in. I'm the super-hip linkster that connects ligaments and tendons to Bone. Ligaments join one bone to the next, while tendons attach the muscles. I also make flat discs to separate Spine's bony rings and stop them from battering and clattering against each other. All in all, it's me that keeps you hanging together as one super-flexible mobile being... 'cos the knee bone's connected to the thigh bone, the thigh bone's connected to the hip bone...

● Elastic cartilage: found in the outer ear
● Fibrocartilage: found in intervertebral discs
● Hyaline cartilage: found in gristle

Cartilage

Skull

■ Musculoskeletal Meatheads

☀ A hard-headed collection of 22 fused bones
☀ This blockhead runs a protection racket for your brain
☀ Has cushioning layers of body tissue beneath the surface

Wah-hey – I'm a total braincase! I'm more of a bonehead than a brainbox, and yet I've got this mentally important job! What were they thinking?

Actually, I'm a pretty sophisticated piece of kit. My bony mask makes a good home for delicate sense organs – ears and eyes to you – and for your gnashers. It's also a blank canvas on which to pin your muscles and your (yes, gorgeous) facial features. Handy hinges operate your jawbone so that you can chew and chat to your heart's content. Eight of my bones are fused together to make your neurocranium. That's the super-hard shell that saves soft Brain from knocks. I'm pretty tough, but no match for concrete. So do me a favour and wear a helmet when you're out riding your bike. Unlike me, it's a no-brainer!

● Fontanelles: soft spots in a baby's skull that make it flexible during birth
● No. of fontanelles in a newborn baby's skull: 6
● Age at which all fontanelles have closed: 2 years

Skull

Spine

■ Musculoskeletal Meatheads

✳ This straight-up character is the backbone of your body
✳ Your lower back, called the lumbar spine, carries most weight
✳ Often the cause of aches and pains in oldsters

Call me proud and upright, straight-laced even, but I've no bone to pick. You see, you can thank me when you stand on your own two feet and hold your head up high.

Reach round to the middle of your back and you'll find my graceful line. I'm a stack of bony rings separated by discs of clever Cartilage. Without him I'd be like a high-rise pile of greasy plates, wobbly and ready to tumble. Instead I'm a tower of strength. At my very top are the axis and atlas bones that allow you to nod for "yes" and shake for "no". At my very bottom (and yours!) is the coccyx – your tail bone. Your ribs hook into me to provide protection for your body's soft organs. And right down my middle is a circular cavity that encloses your vital spinal cord. That takes some nerve! Geddit?

● Name for each individual bone: vertebra (plural vertebrae)
● No. of vertebrae in a human spine: 33
● No. of vertebrae separated by discs: 24

Spine

Chapter 3
Wheezing Windbags and Bloody Busybodies

Put your hands together for your circulatory system. Fronted by Heart and awash with Blood, this is an amazing, fully automatic valeting service for your body. It supplies your body's cells with oxygen and fuel, repairs damage to the skin, protects against microscopic bacterial invasion, defends against disease, *and* carts away your cells' waste products and nasty toxins. Not bad eh? But wait! Save some praise for those gasbags, Lungs, who control your respiratory system. They are in charge of getting oxygen and carbon dioxide out of your blood. It's the ultimate clean-up act, don't miss it!

Heart

Cardiac Muscle

Blood

Lungs

Artery

Capillary

Vein

Heart

■ Wheezing Windbags and Bloody Busybodies

* ✳ A double-action pump that sends blood around your body
* ✳ Cardiac muscle keeps this big-hearted guy pumping
* ✳ Cardiac arrest is when the heart suddenly loses its steady beat

Stop! Listen very carefully... that *lub-dub lub-dub* you hear is me beating out the rhythm of your life. I'm the rootin'-tootin' lubba lubba man and I'm *all* heart!

I pump more than 7000 litres of the red stuff around your body every day. How I do it "beats" me! I sit right at the centre of your chest, tilting slightly to the left. I'm about the size of your fist and I'm protected by your breastbone. With each double pump, my right side pushes oxygen-poor blood out to Lung, who juices it up with life-giving oxygen. At the same time my left side jets oxygen-rich blood around the body, where Cell laps it up. Vein brings the oxygen-poor blood in and Artery carries the good stuff away. I can't repair myself, so you have to take care of me. One way is to exercise – I love a good workout!

* ● Average weight of a human heart: 300 grams (male); 250 grams (female)
* ● Average adult heart rate: 60 beats per minute (at rest)
* ● Capacity of blood pumped: 7200 litres per day

Heart

Cardiac Muscle

Wheezing Windbags and Bloody Busybodies

* A special type of muscle that powers the heart
* Beefy brother of skeletal muscle and smooth muscle
* This Trojan is officially the hardest-working part of your body

Tick, tock, tick, tock. That's my mantra. I am what Heart is made of, the muscle that powers old loverboy's activity. Small, but perfectly formed, I have just one job to do and, believe me, I do it magnificently.

Always pumped up and ready for action, I work without taking a break to keep Blood on the move. You see, if Heart stops beating, Brain can only survive for a few minutes without the life-giving oxygen that Blood brings. And you know what that means... ugh, it makes me *flutter* even to think about it!

In the pumping stakes, I'm second to none. Aided by a small knot of pacemaker cells, I beat a steady rhythm. So you see, it's me that makes that old ticker tick (tock)!

● Proper name: myocardium
● Cardiac muscle cells are called cardiomyocytes
● Frequency: 100,000 beats per day

Cardiac Muscle

Blood

■ Wheezing Windbags and Bloody Busybodies

- ✳ A slippery genius on a nonstop trip around your body
- ✳ A cocktail of plasma, red and white blood cells, and platelets
- ✳ Brings essential supplies to your cells and whisks away the waste

Meet the Red Baron, the king of supply and demand! I run a collection and delivery service for the body, and whaddya know, it's one fluid operation.

The only time you see me is when you cut yourself, so many people don't like me, but there's nothing to be afraid of. I'm a transport coordinator with three handy helpers on board. Red Blood Cell carries oxygen around your body (making me scarlet with pride!). White Blood Cells battle against intruders, helped by tiny platelets. These clever chaps clot on contact with air to form hard, scabby barriers on your skin. Besides oxygen, I cart nutrients, such as fats, proteins, carbohydrates and essential minerals all the way around your body. I even have a sideline in hormones! Ruddy marvellous!

- ● Amount of blood in an average human body: approximately 5 litres
- ● Makeup: plasma – 54.3 %; RBC – 45 %; WBC – 0.7 %
- ● Lifespan of a platelet: 8 to 12 days

Blood

Lungs
■ Wheezing Windbags and Bloody Busybodies

☀ A pair of internal balloon-heads who love to take the air
☀ These blood-soaked lobes are powered by your diaphragm
☀ Breathing is automatic, but can be controlled consciously

Heave-ho! We are the bellow fellows, the inflatables in charge of your body's ventilation. It's a complex task, so take a deep breath – you're gonna need it!

We are two spongy bags, made of minute bubble-shaped chambers of the softest, pinkest, foamiest flesh. These are called alveoli, and it is here that oxygen from the air gets exchanged for carbon dioxide. Here's how it works: your windpipe divides many times over inside us, making millions of microscopic tubes that spread out to all of our alveoli. Capillary carries Blood through the alveoli with Red Blood Cell on board, who picks up the oxygen, ready for transportation to Cell. As he does this, he also deposits Cell's carbon dioxide waste, which you breathe out before breathing in again. And so it goes on.

● Lung capacity: 4.5–6 litres
● No. of alveoli in the human lungs: around 300 million
● Number of breaths in a lifetime: 500 million

Lungs

Artery

Wheezing Windbags and Bloody Busybodies

* A set of pipes and tubes that carry blood away from the heart
* Forms your circulatory system, along with veins and capillaries
* Smaller arteries are called arterioles

You'll have heard that my buddy, Blood, uses a most sophisticated transport network to travel around your body. Well, it's called your circulatory system, and I am very proud to announce, here and now, that I operate a jolly good portion of it.

I run the mainline expressways that lead away from your heart. Mostly my precious cargo is bright-red, oxygen-carrying blood. (The exception, my pulmonary branch line, delivers oxygen-poor blood to your lungs.) Pumped along my length by Heart, Blood is not exactly Mr Speedy, but he *is* under tremendous pressure. That's why I need such thick meaty walls. You'll know if you cut or break my walls, because I can spurt Blood across a room! It's a very draining experience!

● Size of main artery (aorta): 40 cm long and 25 mm wide
● Average width of an artery: 5 mm
● Average thickness of artery wall: 1 mm

Artery

Capillary

Wheezing Windbags and Bloody Busybodies

✴ Micro blood vessels at the end of your branching blood system
✴ These skinny wrigglers join up to your arteries and veins
✴ These tubes refresh the parts that no others can

Tiny and, oh-so-fragile, I thread my way through your body to feed it with life-giving, oxygen-bearing blood. I'm all over you like a rash, from the tips of your fiddlin' fingers to the tops of your twitchin' toes. It's through yours truly that Blood reaches Skin, so you can blame me for all your gushin' blushes. My tiny tubes break easily, which is why you bruise. Gee, I'm a delicate soul!

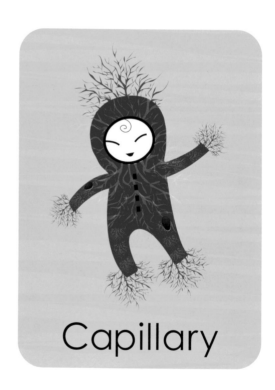

Capillary

● Size: 0.005–0.01 mm
● Thickness of walls: 0.001 mm
● Typical length: 0.7 mm

Vein

Wheezing Windbags and Bloody Busybodies

* This blue-blooded vessel completes your circulatory system
* Has valves to keep the flow going in one direction only
* Although it looks blue, oxygen-poor blood is a dull red colour

Vein

I'm the body's aristocrat – a true blue-blooded grandee. I run the home stretch of your circulatory system, bringing woozy Blood back to Heart. His oxygen-carrying journey is over for the time being, and who can blame him for having the blues? I may not have Artery's heart-felt pressure, but my one-way valves stop exhausted Blood from slipping back down the tube!

* Largest veins: superior and inferior vena cava (attached to the heart)
* Size: 30 mm across
* Blood flow in vena cava: 1 mm per second

Chapter 4
Food Crew and Trash Gang

Please raise your glass for the slurpy, sloppy stars in your food-processing factory – from pulverizing Teeth and liquidizing Saliva, all the way down into churning Stomach and snaking Intestines – these guys operate your amazing digestive system. Working with a handful of deconstruction specialists, such as Enzymes and Gut Bacterium, these munchers get busy extracting nutrients to power your body and get rid of the stuff you no longer need. They're a noisy bunch, this lot – drooling and dribbling, burping and farting, as they guzzle their way through your food. But hey, for them life's just a gas!

Enzymes

Saliva

Teeth

Stomach

Intestines

Smooth Muscle

Gut Bacterium

Gall Bladder

Liver

Kidneys

Bladder

Waste Matter

Enzymes
■ Food Crew and Trash Gang

✳ Wonder proteins that are essential to your body chemistry
✳ Speed up chemical reactions, such as breaking down food
✳ Essential to body chemistry, but remain unchanged in reactions

We are movers and shakers, real smashers that just make things happen. Science bods call us catalysts. That means we speed up your body's chemical reactions without getting used up or altered in the process. Clever eh?

You can find different types of us all over your body. We're right on top of the thousands of chemical processes that occur. We make each one happen faster, while saving on energy. Who is it that cuts your food into simple molecules for your body to use? Yep, it's us! And who helps to make all those proteins that keep you alive? Right again! And because we are unaffected by the reactions we cause, we can repeat the job thousands of times a second. Without us, some of the processes would take so long, your life wouldn't be worth living. Ooh, feel that chemistry!

● No. of known enzyme types: around 4000
● Digestive enzymes: made in the pancreas, salivary glands, stomach, intestines
● Systemic enzymes: found in blood, organs and cells

Enzymes

Saliva

■ Food Crew and Trash Gang

- ☀ This slurpy dribbler softens up food, making it easier to chew
- ☀ Contains mucus, which makes your saliva slimy and stringy
- ☀ The main enzyme in your saliva is a protein called amylase

Boy, oh boy, just smell that… aromas wafting up from the kitchen always get me going. I'm a slippery, slobbery, slimy kinda dude who gets your mouth ready for eating. Ten to one, you drooooool every mealtime!

I'm liquid magic, me. I make your food slushy and easy to swallow. It's me that helps Tongue to taste. I'm packed with Enzymes and get digestion going before food even reaches Stomach. I'm also stuffed full of bacteria. There are millions of these stink balls in your mouth, which can only mean one thing: bad breath! I'm pumped out by six glands – two under your tongue, two beneath your jaw and two under each ear. People tend to make a lot of me when they're excited, spattering friends with flecks when they talk. Please! Say it, don't spray it!

- ● Amount of saliva produced per day: 1–1.5 litres
- ● Amount produced every month: 42 litres
- ● No. of bacteria in your mouth: up to 6 billion

Saliva

Teeth

■ Food Crew and Trash Gang

✳ A team of 32 smilers who grind and shred food
✳ These diamond geezers are the hardest part of your body
✳ Gunky plaque can rot your teeth if you don't brush them daily

Let's hear it for your pearly whites, your gnashers, your chompers. We're talking Teeth, and lots of 'em – your own personal set of grinning, grimacing grinders.

Say cheese and you'll show our handsome, heavy-duty crowns of enamel. Each has a root that slots into a socket in your jawbone and a soft centre packed with blood and nerves. We work as a team. Frontman incisors bite and slice, while their spiky canine neighbours rip and tear. The heavies at the back – pre-molars and molars – chew, grind and crunch their way through anything that's left. We may be tough, but we're not invincible. Mashed-up food and bacteria form a manky, acid-producing coating called plaque. This can dissolve our protective enamel and give you toothache. Ain't that the *trooth*!

● No. of teeth a person has: child 20; adult 32
● Thickness of crown: 2 mm
● Human bite force: 34 kg per cm^2

Teeth

Stomach

■ Food Crew and Trash Gang

☀ A rugby-ball-shaped sack that mashes up your food
☀ Folds in Stomach's lining expand when you scoff a giant meal
☀ Produces gases that make wonderful, loud, smelly burps

Give me some food! Now! I'm one grub-loving guy and there's nothing I like better than going to work on some tasty chow come mealtime. Burp!

I break down food into a nutritious mush called chyme, before passing it on to Intestines. Sure, Teeth, Saliva and Tongue all do a reasonable job up there in the mouth. But I'm a far superior being – a big sloshing, gurgling, glugging vat of enzymes, bacteria and food-dissolving acid. I've got muscle, too, mercilessly squeezing and beating your nosh. And if I can't "stomach" something, I give it the old heave-ho with a swift contraction. Enough of your bloated boasting, I hear you say. OK, OK! After about six hours of my churning, your food begins to look like thick pea soup. My work is done!

● Capacity of a resting stomach: 1–2 litres
● Capacity of a full stomach: 4–5 litres
● Time spent by food in the stomach: 3–6 hours

Stomach

Intestines
■ Food Crew and Trash Gang

- ✳ A 7–9-metre long snaking tube inside your midriff
- ✳ Has two parts: the small intestine and the large intestine
- ✳ Finger-like protrusions, called villi, increase surface area

I'm your body's food-processing and waste-disposal plant. I suck all the juicy goodness from the mushy chyme that Stomach passes on. Waste not, want not!

It all starts in my upper part, the small intestine. I take bile from Liver and enzymes from Pancreas to mix everything up into a salty broth. My twists, turns and hairpin bends are lined with little finger-like villi. They wave about in the slop and the slime, soaking up proteins, minerals, vitamins, sugars, carbohydrates and fat, which seep through my walls into Blood. What's left moves on to my farty parts – the large intestine – where I lap up remaining body salts, minerals and water. There's precious little wastage, I can tell you! In fact, all that's left at the end of the line are some squishy brown lumps headed straight for the U-bend!

- ● No. of villi: around 5 million
- ● Time spent by food in small intestine: 2–4 hours
- ● Time spent by food in large intestine: 12–48 hours

Intestines

Smooth Muscle

■ Food Crew and Trash Gang

- ❋ Fine-textured muscle that works by slow squeezing and pulsing
- ❋ Arranged in layers, with fibres running in a crosswise direction
- ❋ This smooth mover helps your stomach, intestines and bladder

Sleek and sophisticated, I'm a real smooth operator. You'll find me in the darkest depths of your body, where I run an "insides" job for your digestive and urinary systems.

I am the smallest of the muscle brothers and I'm also the most laid back. While Cardiac Muscle works frantically to keep your heart beating, my action is real slow. My fibres are fine and delicate – quite unlike Skeletal Muscle's brawny sinew – and they contract in all directions. I work on my own initiative, scrunching up Intestines' pipes to help digest your food. My slow, pulsating movements ease your nosh through your body. You wouldn't even know I was there. And that's not all I do. I help push babies out during childbirth and I squeeze your bladder to force out your pee – ah, that's a relief!

- ● Official name: visceral muscle
- ● Also known as: involuntary muscle
- ● Length of muscle fibres: 0.2–0.5 mm

Smooth Muscle

Gut Bacterium

■ Food Crew and Trash Gang

✴ Handy alien bug that wriggles and writhes in your intestines
✴ Produces about 2 litres of gas every day as burps and farts
✴ Antibiotics can upset your stomach by killing this guy off

I'm a friendly type who likes to lurk in the gloop and the gloom of your digestive tract. I'm part of an entire alien ecosystem – trillions of single-celled bacterial lifeforms that call your body home. You have more of me inside you than you have cells in your body!

Thankfully, I'm extremely small, so you can carry me and my chums around without any extra effort. I may be a squatter, but boy do you need me. Not only do I aid your digestion, I also produce some essential vitamins and prevent harmful bacteria gaining a foothold. Woe betide any filthy intruder that gets past Stomach's acid when hitching a lift on food and mucky fingers! Breaking down food is a whiffy job – I generate lots of gas in the process. I might have said I was friendly, I never said I was pretty!

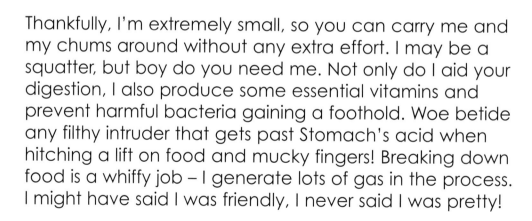

● No. of gut bacteria in a human being: 100 trillion
● No. of different species of gut bacteria: 300–1000
● Volume of bacteria in your poo: 60 %

Gut Bacterium

Gall Bladder

■ Food Crew and Trash Gang

★ This old sourpuss stores bile in readiness to digest your food
★ Bile is a gloopy digestive juice, the colour of fresh-mown grass
★ In the gall bladder, bile becomes concentrated by five times

I am one glorious sac of bitterness in your midriff – a proper bag of bile! In fact, my small pear-shaped tank is home to that self-same acrid digestive fluid. You'll find me just below Liver, in a hollow crafted especially for me.

Bile is also known as gall, which is how I got my name. Liver makes the stuff, producing it even when it is not needed, so I get to store it. Bile goes into the vile mix that Intestines use to break down food. Mostly, bile dissolves the fatty bits, but it also helps to absorb vitamins D, E, K and A in your guts. My own personal moment of glory comes when Stomach releases its mushy chyme. I contract my sac, shooting my goods down to the small intestine. You might taste bile when you vomit. It's really foul and bitter. Some even say it's a "galling" experience!

● Size: 8 cm x 4 cm
● Capacity: 50 ml
● Amount of bile produced by the liver: 1 litre per day

Gall Bladder

Liver

■ Food Crew and Trash Gang

✳ A reddish-brown workhorse in the centre of your body
✳ The body's heaviest internal organ, just pipping Brain to the title
✳ A yellowish tinge to the skin (jaundice) is a sign of liver disease

Wow! Is there *anything* I can't do? The most phenomenal organ in your body, I am a multi-tasker extraordinaire.

Just check this out! I'm a breaker's yard for proteins and worn-out red blood cells, and a rehab unit that scrubs toxins from your blood. I send all my waste to Kidneys. But my speciality has to be digestion. I process and collect nutrients from Blood, which gets piped in to me from your guts. I'm a storehouse for vitamins, iron, and spare carbohydrates and fats. I make vitamin A and control Blood's sugar levels. I also produce gastric juices, called bile, for Intestines. Admit it, I'm pretty amazing, aren't I! It's a lot of work and the heat generated by this powerhouse of activity keeps you nice and toasty. Hey, you can always rely on me to de-"liver"!

● Deepest side: 15 cm
● Weight: about 1.5 kg
● Relative size of human liver: in children, 5 % of body weight; in adults, 2.5 %

Liver

Kidneys
Food Crew and Trash Gang

- ✷ Dark-red, bean-shaped pair of organs in your back
- ✷ The main organs of your urinary system
- ✷ This dynamic duo filter Blood and drain into Bladder

We're a couple of cheeky chappies who love, quite literally, to take the, erm... urine... out of Blood. We clean up your bloodstream and pass all its waste substances and junk on to Bladder.

You'll find us nestled either side of Spine, enjoying the protection of his bony ribs. Sure, we're kidders, but you could never accuse us of shirking. Over the course of any one day we filter your blood around 25 times! Think about it, we spend our entire lives soaked in the ruddy stuff. All the fun takes place in microscopic mini-filters called nephrons. Each of us contains about one million of these guys. They squeeze water and waste out of tiny capillaries and whisk it away down garbage chutes to Bladder. *Bean* there, done that – it's our motto!

- ● Size: about 11 cm high, 6 cm wide, 3 cm deep
- ● Weight: 140–150 g (male); 130–140 g (female)
- ● Total length of nephrons in a kidney: about 65 km

Kidneys

Bladder

■ Food Crew and Trash Gang

- ☀ This is the place where you store your pee
- ☀ Receives liquid waste filtered from the blood by your kidneys
- ☀ You have to learn to control your bladder as a toddler

I'm a pretty simple organ with a rather amazing talent. You see, I have a most incredible capacity (geddit?) to stretch and expand as I fill up with pee. No inflated egos here, I can assure you – I'm puffed up with purpose!

Each of your kidneys has a pipe, called a ureter, through which Kidneys feed me with the liquid waste taken from Blood. My outflow pipe, your urethra, leads away from me and out of your body, taking your pee with it. I have a direct line to Brain. Once I'm around half full of urine, you start to feel that familiar urge to pee. By the time I'm three-quarters full, Brain is well aware that you won't be able to hold on for much longer. Reach full capacity, and you've got screaming desperation – you've just gotta go with the flow!

- ● Bladder capacity: 400–500 ml (adult)
- ● Length of ureter: 15–20 cm
- ● Length of urethra: about 18 cm (male); 4 cm (female)

Bladder

Waste Matter

Food Crew and Trash Gang

- A stinky threesome who are always on the way out
- Straw-coloured wee looks darker when there's less water in it
- Poo needs fibre in the diet to stop it sticking in the gut

Two's company, three's a crowd – and in this case, not a crowd you want to hang out with! We are the toilet trio – urine, faeces and vomit – although you probably know us as wee, poo and puke.

There's only one way food and drink gets into your body, but there are three ways it can come out! Wishy-washy urine is extracted from Blood by Kidneys – two litres a day! She's about 96 per cent water and carries all of Cell's chemical waste and dead red blood cells. Whiffy faeces is a solid sort of chap, carrying those bits of food that your body can't digest. He's jam-packed with bacteria, which is why he smells so yukky. Volatile vomit is more upchuck than waste. This is the food you get to see a second time when Stomach can't take it or has an infection.

- No. of loo rolls used in a lifetime: about 4240
- Lifetime amount of poo: approximately 2865 kg
- Urea: chemical waste found in wee

Waste Matter

Chapter 5
Super Toughs

Get ready to pamper your body's beauty spots, for there's more to this crew than keeping up appearances. They might be good lookers, but your outer bits are also your body's first line of defence and, boy, do these guys take a beating with all the knocks and scrapes that you get them into! As well as the essential barrier services they provide, these dudes help you to stay warm when it's cold and cool when it's hot. From the Hair on your head to high-tech Sweat Gland and your super-sensitive Skin, this is one sophisticated, super-tough team that deserves a whole lotta praise.

Skin

Sweat Gland

Hair

Nails

Skin

■ Super Toughs

✳ This smooth beauty is your body's largest and heaviest organ
✳ Protects against scrapes and blocks germ invasion
✳ Controls temperature and interacts with the outside world

Silky smooth and super-sophisticated, I'm your stretchy sidekick. I am the most hi-tech piece of kit your body has got. A perfect fit, I am a temperature-controlling, hard-wearing, waterproof and self-healing membrane.

And my beauty isn't just skin deep! I'm rammed with hardware below the surface. In just one fingernail-sized patch of me, you'll find a whole metre of blood vessels, a thousand touch-sensitive pressure pads and a hundred oil glands to keep me nice and supple. Besides these are micronerves, sweat glands and hairs galore. I renew my cells in a cycle that replaces my outermost layer in about a month. This means that I shed about 10,000 skin flakes every minute. In fact, there's a sprinkling of dead skin on you right now – makes me tingle to think about it!

● Weight of adult human skin: 3–4 kg
● Average surface area: 1.9 m^2
● Skin thickness: 1 mm at birth; 2 mm as an adult

Skin

Sweat Gland
■ Super Toughs

✺ Slippery secretor lurking beneath Skin's surface
✺ This sporty jock makes sweat and pumps it out of tiny pores
✺ Works hardest when you get hot or emotional

Sweat it out, baby! Embedded in every centimetre of your glorious skin, I produce the juice that keeps your body temperature stable. I'm a cooling customer all right, and just love a good workout!

I make sweat from Blood's watery part, plasma, which is what makes sweat taste salty. And I may make you clammy and red-faced at times, but don't sweat over it, I'm a pretty busy guy. As well as keeping you cool, I offer a fast track for getting toxins out of your body. I also squirt out antibacterial chemicals that keep Skin germ free. So don't you blame your BO on me – I'm doing my best for you, smelly! On top of that, extra glands on your hands help you to get a good hold of things without them slipping from your grasp. Gripping stuff, eh?

● Average no. of sweat glands in a human being: 2 million
● Sweat produced on a hot day: 1.7 litres
● Dangerous water loss through sweating: 5–10 % of body weight (child)

Sweat Gland

Hair

■ Super Toughs

✴ These woolly-headed fibres grow from roots in your skin
✴ Found all over apart from lips, palms of hands and soles of feet
✴ The visible parts of hair are made of non-living keratin

Let's not split hairs, now! There's nothing better than a thick, luxuriant covering of me. And I'm not just talking about the mop up top. Face it, I've got you covered!

I'm all over you. Ever get goosebumps when you're cold or scared? Well that's me standing to attention, hauled up by tiny muscles in your skin. I offer protection (as eyelashes) and warmth (as scalp and body hair).

I'm a softie, but I'm also very tough – I'm made of the protein keratin and am stronger than a copper wire of the same thickness. I grow slowly and can reach 50 to 80 cm long (as head hair) before falling out. That means your oldest hairs are three to five years old and is why you find so many in the plughole! *Hair* today, gone tomorrow!

● Number of hairs on a human head: 130,000 (fair); 105,000 (dark)
● Number of hairs shed: about 100 per day
● Thickness of scalp hair: 0.05 mm

Hair

Nails
Super Toughs

- Little toughnuts found on your fingers and toes
- Made from flat plates of stiff keratin
- Never stop growing and in constant need of trimming

Hard as nails, we're the rough-bitten toughies hangin' off the ends of your fingers and toes. We pinch, scratch, gouge, prise, dig and take the knocks life deals us.

Our roots are our only living parts, buried in the meat of your fidgety digits, and we grow at a snail's pace. The bits you see are as dead as a dodo – flat, stiff plates made of the same stuff as Hair. Your fingers judge the hardness of something when you touch it, by pressing up against us. Without us, your rubbery fingertips would bend right back on themselves (ouch!). We're good for tapping out annoying rhythms – oh, yeah, we've got that nailed. And because we love to get our hands dirty, having the odd nibble of us is a great way to pick up nasty germs. It's nail-bitingly horrid!

- Speed of nail growth: 0.5 mm per week
- Time it takes to replace a lost nail: finger 4–6 months; toe 12–18 months
- Longest nails: 7.51 m (Lee Redmond, USA, grown 1979–2009)

Nails

Chapter 6
Nervous Numbskulls

Crack open that hard headcase of yours, toughnut Skull, and you'll find soft, gooey Brain. It's a bit like whipping the top off your breakfast egg to find it lovely and soft-boiled. But there's a bit more to this clever fella, for he is the leader of a sparky gang of incredible senses. With the help of Nerve Cell and the coordinating genius of Brain's lieutenant, Spinal Cord, the Nervous Numbskulls have the good sense to tell Brain what's happening inside and outside your body. It's thanks to these guys that the world you live in (and not the one in your head) looks, feels, sounds, smells and tastes the way it does.

Brain

Spinal Cord

Eye

Ear

Touch

Nose

Tongue

Brain

Nervous Numbskulls

- This bossy boots controls all your body's processes
- Made from yellowy grey matter and juicy white matter
- Can only function for 8–10 seconds without blood

Peabrain or egghead, I make you the person you are. I am the boss of your thoughts, memories, dreams, hopes, desires and your mysterious sense of yourself. Wrinkled like a walnut, I'm not much to look at, but I rule!

My "head office" is divided into different departments. The brain stem is your life-support system. It controls automatic functions, such as breathing and digestion. The cerebellum is a mini-brain in charge of balance and moving about. At my core, an egg-shaped thalamus processes information from my nervous numbskull pals, while the hypothalamus is important in responses to cold, hunger and pain. But my outer layer – the cerebral cortex – is the real brains of it all. It deals with all those cleverclog functions, such as reading, writing and speaking. Heady stuff, indeed!

- Weight: about 1.4 kg (283 g with all water squeezed out)
- No. of neurons in the brain: 50–100 billion
- No. of dreams in a lifetime: about 100,000

Brain

Spinal Cord
Nervous Numbskulls

* A sparky communicator between your body and your brain
* Has nerve fibres branching out along its length
* Reaction times are fastest in young adults, and slow with age

The king of speed, I'm a zippy-zappy dude who keeps you on your toes. I'm a slinky, slippery type who runs up the middle of your S-shaped spine. I am your body's information highway and, boy, I've got some nerve!

It's through me that Brain gets wind of what your senses are up to. Nerve signals whiz along my length like mini electric pulses and provide a high-speed link that warns of imminent danger. Quick as a flash, Brain sends an order to move and I jolt your reflex reactions into life. This is how you can hit the brakes on your bike before you hit the wall. But I don't always need Brain to get you out of trouble. Say you're about to dip your fingers into boiling water. Well, it's me and me alone who makes you whip them out way before they burn. It's totally electrifying!

* Length: 43–45 cm
* Number of neurons in spinal cord: 1 billion
* Typical reflex reaction time: 150–300 milliseconds

Spinal Cord

Eye
Nervous Numbskulls

* A jelly-filled guy who gives you 3D colour vision
* Eyelids clean the surface using tears from ducts in the corners
* The human eye can see 100,000 to 10 million colours

Clap your eyes on me! I'm one eye-poppin' marvel that's gotta be seen to be believed! I am a true visionary who brings your world into glorious all-colour focus. You can certainly rely on me to see the bigger picture!

I work a bit like a camera, but there's more to me than point and shoot. Thanks to six dedicated muscles, I swivel about to look around (all the better to goggle you with!). My black centre, your pupil, is actually a hole, and your pretty, coloured iris a muscle that I use to control the amount of light that comes in. A lens behind your iris focuses the light on my back wall – your retina – and, hey presto, there's an upside-down image (well, nobody's perfect). Thankfully, Brain flips the image the right way up so you won't think that you're standing on your head!

● Eyeball size: 24.2 mm
● Average time between blinks: 2.8 seconds
● Duration of a blink: 0.1–0.4 seconds

Eye

Ear

Nervous Numbskulls

* Waxy chap whose good vibrations allow you to hear sound
* Picks up on both the direction and the distance of a sound
* Fluid-filled canals deep in your ears help you to keep balance

I'm all ears and totally wired for sound! You might think my flaps and folds and sticky-out bits look weird, but believe me, my strangest bits are deep inside. Listen up and I'll show you around.

When a sound gets made, my shell-like bits channel vibrations in the air into your ear hole. These beat a tattoo on my eardrum – a skin stretched tight over the hole – which in turn passes to the three smallest bones in your body: the hammer, anvil and stirrup. These rhythm-lovers pass the sound on to the cochlea. This is a tube filled with fluid. Each vibration sends a ripple through the fluid, which makes microscopic hairs twitch and quiver. In doing so, they send nerve impulses to Brain, who interprets the signals as sound, giving you a bit of an earful!

● Smallest bone (stirrup): 3 mm long
● Number of hairs in cochlea: 3500 (inner hair cells); 12,000 (outer hair cells)
● Range of human hearing: 20 Hz to 20,000 Hz

Ear

Touch
Nervous Numbskulls

🌟 Super-detector of pressure, temperature, texture and moisture
🌟 Pain sensors spread all over your skin warn you of danger
🌟 Referred to by science bods as your somatosensory system

I'm "sense"-ational. Can't you just *feeeel* my vibes?
I work hand in hand with Skin and am spread out in a
network of complicated sensors, receptors and triggers.
Go on, have a poke! I'm all wriggles, tickles and jiggles.

But I do have a serious side. Close to the surface of your
hairless bits are very sensitive sensors. They detect even
the lightest of touches and send early-warning messages
to Brain whenever you come too close to something
that might cause you harm. I also have deeper-lying
pressure receptors that respond to heavy touch. These
help you figure out how hard an object is. It's down to
these little fellows that you know instinctively how much
pressure to use – or not – when holding something robust
(a rock) or something fragile (a kitten). How touching!

● Number of receptors in the human hand: 17,000
● Most sensitive areas: fingertips, lips and tip of the tongue
● Least sensitive area: middle of the back

Touch

Nose

▪ Nervous Numbskulls

- ☀ Hoity-toity character with a famous sense of smell
- ☀ Gets your mouth watering before you even get food to your lips
- ☀ Your sense of smell is properly called olfaction

Conk? Hooter? What insults! Deep inside me (and out of the reach of rootling fingers) is a little patch of chemical sensors. Without these, you'd not be able to smell anything or taste your food. Just imagine! But that's not all I do. Tiny hairs snag grime on its way into your body. My mucus mops it up and the hairs sweep the gunk to the back of the throat. "Snot" bad, eh?

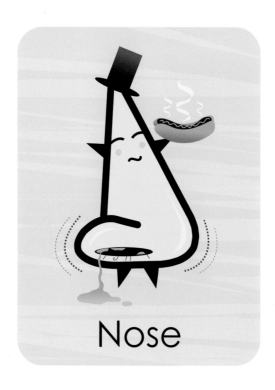

Nose

- ● Wind speed of a sneeze: 30 m/s
- ● No. of smell receptors in human nose: 12 million
- ● No. of smell receptors in a bloodhound dog's nose: 4 billion

Tongue

Nervous Numbskulls

- ✳ An acrobat with 16 separate muscles
- ✳ Helps you find your way around language
- ✳ Can get covered in smelly bacteria, giving you bad breath

Tongue

A man of taste, I tell Brain what's yummy or yucky when you eat. My surface is covered with thousands of lumps, called taste buds. These little critters detect sweet, sour, salty, bitter and umami (a savoury meatiness) in your food. But, hey, there's more. Thanks to my muscular make-up I can slurp food around your mouth and let you talk ten to the dozen. There's no licking me!

- ● Number of taste buds on the tongue: 9,000
- ● Height of a taste bud: 0.05–0.1 mm
- ● Number of receptors on each taste bud: 50–150

Chapter 7
Team Players and System Admin

This little band of softies may leave a wet impression, but – respect, please – they don't have the most glamorous jobs. They drain out tired cells, mop up slop, and clean away toxins, poisons and tiny living invaders. Someone has to do it, and like all service staff, these guys are pretty indispensible. Team Immunity fights infections and helps prevent future illness. These guys operate hand in hand with Lymph's incredible system to keep you spick and span. Unlike your heart, Lymph doesn't use a pump to get moving. Instead, the slippy stuff slides through tiny tubes powered by muscle contractions. Heave-ho!

Lymph

Team Immunity

Spleen

Hormones

Pancreas

Gland Gang

Lymph
Team Players and System Admin

* Watery liquid with the same salty make-up as blood plasma
* Runs all over your body with Team Immunity on board
* Has its own system of tubes, but no heart-like pump

I'm pretty wet, me. A real drip, in fact! I'm the pale liquid that oozes out from cuts and spots before they start to bleed. I slip and slide between your body tissues to provide a cleansing service for Cell.

I'm made up of water, blood plasma and white blood cells. As Blood squeezes through Capillary, I filter out and enter my own lymphatic vessels. I trickle around your cells, whisking away waste and germs. Team Immunity come along for the ride, looking to combat any invading bugs. My lymph nodes are like field hospitals, removing the bodies of those who fall as the battle rages. These beany lumps double in size and become sore to touch when you are fighting an illness. Job done, I drain back into your bloodstream in your chest. Drip, drip, drip…

● Amount of lymph in body: 1–2 litres
● No. of lymph nodes in body: 500
● Lymph node size: 1–20 mm

Lymph

Team Immunity
■ Team Players and System Admin

✳ White blood cell duo that keeps you sickness-free
✳ Produces antibodies that lock on to germs to neutralize them
✳ Gives you resistance – immunity – to bugs in the future

We're a highly trained special ops team that tracks down invaders in your bloodstream. You know the sort: bacteria, nasty germs, viruses and parasites – filth, the lot of 'em. Always on patrol, B-Cell spots foreign bodies encountered in the past and marks them with his antibodies. Then Killer T-Cell moves in to finish the job. Immunity with impunity, that's our motto!

Team Immunity

● Different types of white blood cell (leucocyte) in your body: 5
● Proper name for B- and T-cell: lymphocyte
● Healthy white blood cell count: 4 million to 11 million per 1 ml of blood

Spleen

Team Players and System Admin

* Soft, purple clean-up guy for your immune system
* A mass of lymphatic tissue, left of, and below, the diaphragm
* Plumbed in to your bloodstream and your lymphatic system

Spleen

Emphatically lymphatic, I whisk away all the debris and decay that Team Immunity leaves in the wake of its destruction. I'm talking antibody-splurged parasites and toothless bacteria – not pretty! I sweep up old red blood cells while I'm about it. At the same time, I house half your body's monocytes – white blood cells that deal with infection. I've gotta be "spleen" to be believed!

● Size of adult spleen: 11 cm long
● Weight of adult spleen: 150 g
● Position in body: betweeen 9th and 12th thoracic ribs

Hormones

Team Players and System Admin

* Regulate your body processes and control growth
* Govern your emotions and can sometimes rage!
* Part of the endocrine system, along with the Gland Gang

A bustling bunch of errand boys, we are your body's chemical messengers. Released by the Gland Gang, we whiz around your body activating, stimulating and regulating all kinds of activity.

Need a little more zip in your heels? We know where to get it. Feeling the stress of a situation? We've got just the thing to help you cope. We get a bad press from teenagers and pregnant women, whose OTT behaviour gets blamed on us, but take a look at everything we do. We regulate your metabolism and manage your energy and your sleep patterns. We organize how you add extra cells to your body so that you grow, and help you mature into an adult. There's so much going on, who can blame us for raging from time to time. It's all part of growing up!

● Number of different hormones in body: 50–100
● Thyroid hormone: regulates metabolism
● Adrenalin: increases heart and respiratory rate

Hormones

Pancreas

Team Players and System Admin

* Digestive organ that works in the shade of mighty Liver
* Produces digestive juices laced with corrosive chemicals
* A Gland Gang member that produces insulin and glucagon

Slim and sock-shaped (although without the holes and the pong), I am a factory for carbohydrate-mulching, protein-munching and fat-guzzling enzymes.

My "hot sauce" pancreatic juices contain about fifteen powerful chemicals that make short work of your burger and chips. These are piped through my pancreatic ducts into Intestines' upper parts. Besides my digestive work, I have the important task of regulating your blood sugar levels: too high and Heart and Kidney might suffer; too low and Brain could be starved of fuel. Enter insulin and glucagon, a balancing act of distinction. Insulin tells Liver to store excess sugar in your blood after eating, while glucagon gets Liver to release its stocks when levels are low. Gee, they're my hormone heroes!

● Weight: about 0.1 kg
● Length: about 15 cm
● Amount of pancreatic juices produced: 1.5 litres per day

Pancreas

Gland Gang
Team Players and System Admin

* The floppy backbone of your endocrine system
* Produce hormones and pump them straight into your blood
* Pituitary runs the show, taking orders directly from Brain

We are a jolly bunch of squidgy body bits. We might not be much to look at, but with *gland* master pituitary at the helm, we run a tight ship. Come and meet the team.

Tiny pineal is the size of a rice grain. Hidden deep inside Brain, this diminuitive genius controls your sleep-wake cycle with melatonin. Butterfly-shaped thyroid in your neck drives Cell to work faster and harder. Adrenal bonnets on top of Kidneys produce adrenalin when you're scared and cortisol when you're excited. You've already met Pancreas. Ovary (in girls) and testes (in boys) are the source of your womanhood and manliness. Pituitary is amazing, producing hormones that control your growth while managing to run the entire operation. Shaped like a small bean, this little critter lives in your head.

● Pineal gland size: 5–8 mm
● Thyroid gland weight: 10–30 g
● No. of important hormones: about 67

Gland Gang

Index

L
Liver 4, 20, 72, 78, 80, 120
Lungs 38, 48, 50, 56
Lymph 112, 114

M
Man 6, 8
Mitochondrion 18
muscles 34, 40, 52, 74, 127

N
Nails 4, 96
Nerve Cell 26, 98
Nose 42, 110

O
Osteoblast 32, 38

P
Pancreas 64, 72, 120, 122
Protein 19, 40, 64, 66, 72, 80

R
Red Blood Cell 28, 54, 56,
 80, 86, 117

S
Saliva 62, 64, 66, 70
Skeletal Muscle 36, 40, 52,
 74

Skin 4, 34, 48, 60, 88, 90,
 92, 94, 108
Skull 8, 36, 38, 44
Smooth Muscle 40, 52, 74
Sperm 8, 22
Spinal Cord 46, 98, 102
Spine 36, 42, 46, 82, 102
Spleen 117
Stem Cell 20, 32
Stomach 64, 66, 70, 72, 74,
 76, 78, 86
Sweat Gland 88, 90, 92

T
Team Immunity 112, 114,
 116, 117
Teeth 44, 62, 68, 70
Tongue 66, 70, 108, 111
Touch 108

V
Vein 50, 58, 60, 61
Vesalius, Andreas 4

W
Waste Matter 86
White Blood Cells 30, 54,
 114, 116, 117
Woman 6, 8, 24

Glossary

Amino acids These molecules are the building blocks of proteins. Your body produces 14 of the 22 amino acids it needs and takes the rest from food.

Antibodies Part of your immune system, these are produced by B-cells to combat viruses and bacteria.

Circulatory system The network of arteries and veins that carries blood around your body. Also called the cardiovascular system.

Collagen Connective body tissue, made up of protein. It can also be found in your muscles.

Diaphragm A sheet of muscle below your lungs. It contracts when you breathe in and relaxes when you breathe out.

Digestive system The body system involved in breaking down your food.

Endocrine system A system of glands that produce hormones to control and regulate your metabolism.

Fertilization When a man's sperm combines with a woman's egg to create a new being.

Genome The sum total of all your genes.

Gestation The period of time that a baby lives inside a pregnant woman (35–40 weeks in humans).

Immune system The body system involved in resisting illness and infection.

Lymphatic system A network of ducts and vessels that transport lymph around your body.

Membrane A stretchy lining made from body tissue. Encases body bits and organs or forms a barrier between them.

Metabolism All the chemical reactions that need to happen to keep you alive. This includes reactions that build, maintain and destroy your body's cells, as well as those that convert energy. Regulated by enzymes.

Mucus A slippery, slimy substance produced by the nose, stomach, lungs and throat. It protects against, and washes away, irritants.

Muscular system The body system involved with movement.

Glossary

Nervous system A network of nerves and neurons that transmits signals around your body and allows your brain to communicate with the rest of the body.

Nucleus The central part of a cell, where the DNA chromosomes are kept; a control centre for cell chemistry.

Plasma The "watery" part of blood; yellowy coloured and without red blood cells.

Platelets Cells without a nucleus; carried in the blood, they help it to clot.

Reproductive system The parts of the human body that make sex cells and are involved with making babies.

Respiratory system The body system involved in breathing, centred on the lungs.

Skeletal system The system of body tissues that forms a rigid framework.

Water The number one chemical in your body. It makes up 75 per cent of a baby's body and 57 per cent of an average male adult, and nothing could happen without it.